The Piano Works of Rachmaninoff

Volume V • Sonatas: Op. 28 & Op. 36
(Piano Solo)

Alfred's Classic Editions

Alfred

The Piano Works of Rachmaninoff

Volume V • Sonatas: Op. 28 & Op. 36
(Piano Solo)

Alfred's Classic Editions

Table of Contents

St. Basil's Cathedral in Moscow, **courtesy of PhotoDisc**

About the Recording

The CD recordings within this book do not adhere specifically to the tempo, dynamic, and phrasing indications included in the music. Because music is an art form and not a science, many great pianists, conductors, and even composers vary their interpretations and performances as they gain insight into a work. Listening to a fine interpretation of a work is beneficial; however, a well-rounded performance is balanced by the pianist's musicality as well as stylistically correct performance practices.

All tracks performed by İdil Biret

Second Edition
Copyright © MCMLXXXIX BELWIN-MILLS PUBLISHING CORP.
All Rights Controlled and Administered by ALFRED PUBLISHING CO., INC.
All Rights Reserved
ISBN-10: 0-7390-4457-5
ISBN-13: 978-0-7390-4457-5

Sonata No. 1 in D Minor
(1907)
I.

Sergei Rachmaninoff (1873–1943)
Op. 28

poco a poco cresc. e agitato

Moderato

II.

poco a poco cresc.

III.

Allegro moderato

44

57

à M. Pressmann

Sonata No. 2 in B-flat Minor
(1913)

I.

Sergei Rachmaninoff (1873–1943)

Op. 36

II.

Tempo I

76

III.

82

Tempo rubato